The Simple Air Fryer Cookbook

Learn How to Make Simple and Delicious Recipes with Your Air Fryer on a Budget

Linda Wang

© **Copyright 2021 by Linda Wang - All rights reserved.**

The content contained within this book may not be reproduced, duplicated or transmitted without direct written permission from the author or the publisher.
Under no circumstances will any blame or legal responsibility be held against the publisher, or author, for any damages, reparation, or monetary loss due to the information contained within this book. Either directly or indirectly.

Legal Notice:
This book is copyright protected. This book is only for personal use. You cannot amend, distribute, sell, use, quote or paraphrase any part, or the content within this book, without the consent of the author or publisher.

Disclaimer Notice:
Please note the information contained within this document is for educational and entertainment purposes only. All effort has been executed to present accurate, up to date, and reliable, complete information. No warranties of any kind are declared or implied. Readers acknowledge that the author is not engaging in the rendering of legal, financial, medical or professional advice. The content within this book has been derived from various sources. Please consult a licensed professional before attempting any techniques outlined in this book.
By reading this document, the reader agrees that under no circumstances is the author responsible for any losses, direct or indirect, which are incurred as a result of the use of information contained within this document, including, but not limited to, — errors, omissions, or inaccuracies.

TABLE OF CONTENTS

INTRODUCTION 1

Breakfast Egg Tomato 5

Egg, Bacon and Cheese Roll Ups 7

Sausage Bacon Fandango 9

Vanilla Oatmeal 11

Delicious Broccoli Bites with Hot Sauce 13

Creamy Tuna Cakes 15

Wasabi Crab Cakes 17

Air Fried Tuna Salad Bites 19

Air-Fried Crab Sticks 21

Coconut Shrimp 23

Fish & Chips 25

Shrimp and Corn 27

Jerk Chicken, Pineapple and Veggie Kabobs 28

Curried Chicken 30

Chicken with Carrots 32

Delicious Chicken Burgers 34

Duck Rolls 37

Turkey Meatloaf 39

Fried Chicken Thighs 41

Sesame Chicken 43

- Meatloaf ... 45
- Chili Garlic Chicken Wings ... 47
- Pesto Coated Rack of Lamb ... 49
- Beef and Veggie Spring Rolls ... 51
- Ham Pinwheels ... 53
- Vegetable Cane ... 55
- Basil Beef Roast ... 57
- Lamb Loin Chops with Garlic ... 58
- Fried Pork ... 60
- Roasted Veggie Bowl ... 62
- Wine Infused Mushrooms ... 64
- Cheesy Spinach ... 66
- Grilled Chicken with Bold Dressing ... 68
- Indian Spiced Chicken, Eggplant, and Tomato Skewers ... 70
- Grilled Chicken with Shishito Peppers ... 72
- Stuffed Mushrooms with Sour Cream ... 73
- Air Fried Chicken Tenders ... 75
- French Toast Bites ... 77
- Currant Cream ... 79
- Marshmallow Pastries ... 80
- Double Layer Lemon Bars ... 82
- Chocolate Mug Cake ... 84
- Blueberry Cake ... 86

Cinnamon Rolls 88

Raspberry-Coconut Cupcake 89

Apple-Toffee Upside-Down Cake 91

Strawberry Pop Tarts 93

Gluten Free Chocó Lava Cake 95

Cinnamon Mug Cake 97

Raspberry Bites 99

NOTES 101

INTRODUCTION

An Air Fryer is a magic revolutionized kitchen appliance that helps you fry with less or even no oil at all. This kind of product applies Rapid Air technology, which offers a new way to fry with less oil. This new invention cooks food through the circulation of superheated air and generates 80% low-fat food. Although the food is fried with less oil, you don't need to worry as the food processed by the Air Fryer still has the same taste like the food fried using the deep-frying method.

This technology uses a superheated element, which radiates heat close to the food and an exhaust fan in its lid to circulate airflow. An Air Fryer ensures that the food processed is cooked completely. The exhaust fan located at the top of the cooking chamber helps the food get the same heating temperature in every part quickly, resulting in a cooked food of better and healthier quality. Besides, cooking with an Air Fryer is also suitable for those individuals which are too busy or do not have enough time. For example, an Air Fryer only needs half a spoonful of oil and takes 10 minutes to serve a medium bowl of crispy French fries.

In addition to serving healthier food, an Air Fryer also provides some other benefits to you. Since an Air Fryer helps you fry using less oil or without oil for some kind of food, it automatically reduces the fat and cholesterol content in food. Indeed, no one will refuse to enjoy fried food without worrying about the greasy and fat content. Having fried food with no guilt is one of the pleasures of life. Besides having low fat and cholesterol, you save some amount of money by consuming oil sparingly, which can be used for other needs. An Air Fryer also can reheat your food. Sometimes, when you have fried leftover and you reheat it, it will usually serve reheated greasy food with some addition of unhealthy reuse oil. Undoubtedly, the saturated fat in the fried food gets worse because of this process. An Air Fryer helps you reheat your food without being afraid of extra oils that the food may absorb. Fried bananas, fish and chips, nuggets, or even fried chicken can be reheated to become as warm and crispy as they were before by using an Air Fryer.

Some people may think that spending some amount of money to buy a fryer is wasteful. I dare to say that they are wrong because an Air Fryer is not only used to fry. It is a sophisticated multi-function appliance since it also helps you to roast chicken, make steak, grill fish, and even bake a cake. With a built-in air filter, an Air Fryer filters the air and saves your kitchen from smoke and grease.

An air Fryer is really a new innovative method of cooking. Grab it fast and welcome to a clean and healthy kitchen.

Breakfast Egg Tomato

Preparation Time: 10 minutes

Cooking Time: 24 minutes

Serve: 2

Ingredients:

- 2 eggs
- 2 large fresh tomatoes
- 1 tsp fresh parsley

- Pepper
- Salt

Directions:

1. Preheat the air fryer to 325 °F.
2. Cut off the top of a tomato and spoon out the tomato innards.
3. Break the egg in each tomato and place in air fryer basket and cook for 24 minutes.
4. Season with parsley, pepper, and salt.
5. Serve and enjoy.

Nutrition:

Calories 95, Fat 5 g, Carbohydrates 7.5 g, Sugar 5.1 g, Protein 7 g, Cholesterol 164 mg

Egg, Bacon and Cheese Roll Ups

Preparation Time: 30 minutes

Servings: 4

Ingredients:

- ½ medium green bell pepper; seeded and chopped
- ¼ cup chopped onion
- 12 slices sugar-free bacon.
- 6 large eggs.
- 1 cup shredded sharp Cheddar cheese.
- ½ cup mild salsa, for dipping
- 2 tbsp. unsalted butter.

Directions:

1. In a medium skillet over medium heat, melt butter. Add onion and pepper to the skillet and sauté until fragrant and onions are translucent, about 3 minutes
2. Whisk eggs in a small bowl and pour into skillet. Scramble eggs with onions and peppers until

fluffy and fully cooked, about 5 minutes. Remove from heat and set aside

3. On work surface, place three slices of bacon side by side, overlapping about ¼-inch. Place ¼ cup scrambled eggs in a heap on the side closest to you and sprinkle ¼ cup cheese on top of the eggs.
4. Tightly roll the bacon around the eggs and secure the seam with a toothpick if necessary. Place each roll into the air fryer basket
5. Adjust the temperature to 350 Degrees F and set the timer for 15 minutes. Rotate the rolls halfway through the cooking time. Bacon will be brown and crispy when completely cooked. Serve immediately with salsa for dipping.

Nutrition:

Calories: 460; Protein: 28.2g; Fiber: 0.8g; Fat: 31.7g; Carbs: 6.1g

Sausage Bacon Fandango

Preparation Time: 5 minutes

Cooking Time: 20 minutes

Servings: 4

Ingredients:

- 8 chicken sausages
- 8 bacon slices
- 4 eggs

- Salt and black pepper, to taste

Directions:

1. Preheat the Air fryer to 320 degrees F and grease 4 ramekins lightly.
2. Place bacon slices and sausages in the Air fryer basket.
3. Cook for about 10 minutes and crack 1 egg in each prepared ramekin.
4. Season with salt and black pepper and cook for about 10 more minutes.
5. Divide bacon slices and sausages in serving plates.
6. Place 1 egg in each plate and serve warm.

Nutrition:

Calories: 287, Fat: 21.5g, Carbs: 0.9g, Sugar: 0.3g, Protein: 21.4g, Sodium: 1007mg

Vanilla Oatmeal

Preparation Time: 22 minutes

Servings: 4

Ingredients:

- 1 cup milk
- 1 cup steel cut oats
- 2½ cups water

- 2 tsp. vanilla extract
- 2 tbsp. brown sugar

Directions:

1. In a pan that fits your air fryer, mix all ingredients and stir well. Place the pan in your air fryer and cook at 360 °F for 17 minutes. Divide into bowls and serve

Delicious Broccoli Bites with Hot Sauce

Preparation Time: 20 minutes

Servings: 6

Ingredients:

For the Broccoli Bites:

- 1 medium-sized head broccoli; broken into florets
- 1/2 teaspoon lemon zest; freshly grated
- 1/2 teaspoon hot paprika
- 1/3 teaspoon fine sea salt
- 1 teaspoon shallot powder
- 1 teaspoon porcini powder
- 1/2 teaspoon granulated garlic
- 1/3 teaspoon celery seeds
- 1 ½ tablespoons olive oil

For the Hot Sauce:

- 1/2 cup tomato sauce
- 1 tablespoon balsamic vinegar
- 3 tablespoons brown sugar
- 1/2 teaspoon ground allspice

Directions:

1. Toss all the ingredients for the broccoli bites in a mixing bowl; covering the broccoli florets on all sides.
2. Cook them in the preheated Air Fryer at 360 degrees for 13 to 15 minutes.
3. In the meantime; mix all ingredients for the hot sauce.
4. Pause your Air Fryer; mix the broccoli with the prepared sauce and cook for further 3 minutes.

Creamy Tuna Cakes

Preparation Time: 15 minutes

Cooking Time: 15 minutes

Servings: 4

Ingredients:

- 2: 6-ouncescans tuna, drained
- 1½ tablespoons mayonnaise
- 1 tablespoon fresh lemon juice
- 1½ tablespoon almond flour
- 1 teaspoon dried dill
- 1 teaspoon garlic powder
- ½ teaspoon onion powder
- Pinch of salt and ground black pepper

Directions:

1. Preheat the Air fryer to 400 degrees F and grease an Air fryer basket.
2. Mix the tuna, mayonnaise, almond flour, lemon juice, dill, and spices in a large bowl.

3. Make 4 equal-sized patties from the mixture and arrange in the Air fryer basket.
4. Cook for about 10 minutes and flip the sides.
5. Cook for 5 more minutes and dish out the tuna cakes in serving plates to serve warm.

Nutrition:

Calories: 200, Fat: 10.1g, Carbohydrates: 2.9g, Sugar: 0.8g, Protein: 23.4g, Sodium: 122mg

Wasabi Crab Cakes

Preparation Time: 20 minutes

Cooking Time: 24 minutes

Servings: 6

Ingredients:

- 3 scallions, finely chopped
- 2 large egg whites
- 1 celery rib, finely chopped
- 1/3 cup plus ½ cup dry breadcrumbs, divided
- 1½ cups lump crab meat, drained
- 3 tablespoons mayonnaise
- 1 medium sweet red pepper, finely chopped
- ¼ teaspoon prepared wasabi
- Salt to taste

Directions:

1. Preheat the Air fryer to 375 degrees F and grease an Air fryer basket.

2. Mix scallions, red pepper, celery, 1/3 cup of breadcrumbs, egg whites, mayonnaise, wasabi, and salt in a large bowl.
3. Fold in the crab meat gently and mix well.
4. Place the remaining breadcrumbs in another bowl.
5. Make ¾-inch thick patties from the mixture and arrange half of the patties into the Air fryer.
6. Cook for about 12 minutes, flipping once halfway through and repeat with the remaining patties.
7. Dish out and serve warm.

Nutrition:

Calories: 112, Fat: 4g, Carbohydrates: 15.5g, Sugar: 2.7g, Protein: 4.9g, Sodium: 253mg

Air Fried Tuna Salad Bites

Preparation Time: 17 minutes

Servings: 12 bites

Ingredients:

- 1: 10-oz.can tuna, drained
- ½ cup blanched finely ground almond flour,

divided.
- 1 stalk celery; chopped
- ¼ cup full-fat mayonnaise
- 1 medium avocado; peeled, pitted and mashed
- 2 tsp. coconut oil

Directions:

1. Take a large bowl, mix tuna, mayonnaise, celery and mashed avocado. Form the mixture into balls.
2. Roll balls in almond flour and spritz with coconut oil. Place balls into the air fryer basket.
3. Adjust the temperature to 400 Degrees F and set the timer for 7 minutes.
4. Gently turn tuna bites after 5 minutes. Serve warm.

Nutrition:

Calories: 323; Protein: 17.3g; Fiber: 4.0g; Fat: 25.4g; Carbs: 6.3g

Air-Fried Crab Sticks

Preparation time: 10 minutes

Servings: 2-3

Ingredients:

- Crab sticks: 1 package
- Cooking oil spray: as needed

Directions:

1. Take each of the sticks out of the package and unroll until flat. Tear the sheets into thirds.
2. Arrange them on a plate and lightly spritz using cooking spray. Set the timer for 10 minutes.
3. Note: If you shred the crab meat; you can cut the time in half, but they will also easily fall through the holes in the basket.

Coconut Shrimp

Preparation time: 20 minutes

Servings: 3

Ingredients:

- Shrimp: 12 large
- Coconut – unsweetened & dried: 1 cup
- Gluten-free breadcrumbs: 1 cup
- Gluten-free flour: 1 cup

- Egg white: 1 cup
- Cornstarch: 1 tbsp.

Directions:
1. Set the Air Fryer to 350º Fahrenheit.
2. Select a shallow platter and combine coconut and the breadcrumbs.
3. In another bowl, mix the flour and cornstarch. Break the egg into a small bowl.
4. Coat the shrimp with the egg white, flour, and lastly the breadcrumbs.
5. Place in the fryer basket and fry for 10 minutes.
6. Serve with your favorite sides or as a quick snack.

Fish & Chips

Preparation time: 10 minutes

Servings: 4

Ingredients:

- Catfish fillets or similar fish: 2
- Wholemeal bread for breadcrumbs: 3 slices
- Medium beaten egg: 1
- Bag tortilla chips: 0.88 oz. or approximately/25g
- Juice and rind of 1 lemon

- Pepper and salt
- Parsley: 1 tbsp.

Directions:

1. Warm the fryer before baking time to reach 356º Fahrenheit.
2. Zest and juice the lemon.
3. Slice the fillets into four pieces ready for cooking. Season each one with the lemon juice and set aside for a few minutes.
4. Use a food processor to mix the tortillas, parsley, pepper, breadcrumbs, and lemon zest.
5. Whisk the egg and egg wash the fish. Run it through the crumb mixture. Place them onto the baking tray and cook until crispy.
6. Preparation time is ten minutes with a total cooking time of fifteen minutes; so, wait patiently to enjoy.

Shrimp and Corn

Preparation Time: 20 minutes

Servings: 4

Ingredients:

- 1½ lbs. shrimp; peeled and deveined
- 2 cups corn
- 1/4 cup chicken stock
- 2 sweet onions; cut into wedges
- 1 tbsp. old bay seasoning
- 1 tsp. red pepper flakes; crushed
- A drizzle of olive oil
- 8 garlic cloves; crushed
- Salt and black pepper to taste

Directions:

1. Grease a pan that fits your air fryer with the oil.
2. Add all other ingredients to the oiled pan and toss well
3. Place the pan in the fryer and cook at 390°F for 10 minutes. Divide everything into bowls and serve

Jerk Chicken, Pineapple and Veggie Kabobs

Preparation Time: 20 minutes

Cooking Time: 18 minutes

Servings: 8

Ingredients:

- 8: 4-ounces boneless, skinless chicken thigh fillets, trimmed and cut into cubes
- 2 large zucchinis, sliced
- 8 ounces white mushrooms, stems removed
- 1: 20-ounces can pineapple chunks, drained
- 1 tablespoon jerk seasoning
- Wooden skewers, presoaked
- 1 tablespoon jerk sauce
- Salt and black pepper, to taste

Directions:

1. Preheat the Air fryer to 370 degrees F and grease an Air fryer pan.
2. Mix the chicken cubes and jerk seasoning in a

bowl.

3. Season the zucchini slices and mushrooms evenly with salt and black pepper.
4. Thread chicken, zucchinis, mushrooms and pineapple chunks onto presoaked wooden skewers.
5. Transfer half of the skewers in the Air fryer pan and cook for about 9 minutes.
6. Repeat with the remaining mixture and dish out to serve hot.

Nutrition:

Calories: 274, Fat: 8.7g, Carbohydrates: 14.1g, Sugar: 9.9g, Protein: 35.1g, Sodium: 150mg

Curried Chicken

Preparation Time: 15 minutes

Cooking Time: 18 minutes

Servings: 3

Ingredients:

- 1 pound boneless chicken, cubed
- 1 medium yellow onion, thinly sliced
- ½ tablespoon cornstarch
- 1 egg
- ½ cup evaporated milk
- 1 tablespoon light soy sauce
- 2 tablespoons olive oil
- 5 curry leaves
- 3 teaspoons garlic, minced
- 1 teaspoon fresh ginger, grated
- 1 teaspoon curry powder
- 1 tablespoon chili sauce
- 1 teaspoon sugar
- Salt and black pepper, as required

Directions:

1. Preheat the Air fryer to 390 degrees F and grease an Air fryer basket.
2. Mix the chicken cubes, soy sauce, cornstarch and egg in a bowl and keep aside for about 1 hour.
3. Arrange the chicken cubes into the Air Fryer basket and cook for about 10 minutes.
4. Heat olive oil in a medium skillet and add onion, green chili, garlic, ginger, and curry leaves.
5. Sauté for about 4 minutes and stir in the chicken cubes, curry powder, chili sauce, sugar, salt, and black pepper.
6. Mix well and add the evaporated milk.
7. Cook for about 4 minutes and dish out the chicken mixture into a serving bowl to serve.

Nutrition:

Calories: 363, Fat: 19g, Carbohydrates: 10g, Sugar: 0.8g, Protein: 37.1g, Sodium: 789mg

Chicken with Carrots

Preparation Time: 15 minutes

Cooking Time: 25 minutes

Servings: 2

- **Ingredients:**
- 1 carrot, peeled and thinly sliced
- 2: 4-ounceschicken breast halves
- 2 tablespoons butter
- 1 tablespoon fresh rosemary, chopped
- Salt and black pepper, as required
- 2 tablespoons fresh lemon juice

Directions:
1. Preheat the Air fryer to 375 degrees F and grease an Air fryer basket.
2. Place 2 square-shaped parchment papers onto a smooth surface and arrange carrot slices evenly in the center of each parchment paper.

3. Drizzle ½ tablespoon of butter over carrot slices and season with salt and black pepper.
4. Layer with chicken breasts and top with rosemary, lemon juice and remaining butter.
5. Fold the parchment paper on all sides and transfer into the Air fryer.
6. Cook for about 25 minutes and dish out in a serving platter to serve.

Nutrition:

Calories: 339, Fats: 20.3g, Carbohydrates: 4.4g, Sugar: 1.8g, Proteins: 33.4g, Sodium: 2822mg

Delicious Chicken Burgers

Preparation Time: 20 minutes

Cooking Time: 30 minutes

Servings: 4

Ingredients:

- 4 boneless, skinless chicken breasts
- 2 eggs
- 1 ¾ ounces plain flour

- 4 hamburger buns, split and toasted
- 4 mozzarella cheese slices
- 1 teaspoon mustard powder
- ½ teaspoon paprika
- 1 teaspoon Worcestershire sauce
- ¼ teaspoon dried parsley
- ¼ teaspoon dried tarragon
- ¼ teaspoon dried oregano
- 1 teaspoon dried garlic
- 1 teaspoon chicken seasoning
- ½ teaspoon cayenne pepper
- Salt and black pepper, as required

Directions:

1. Preheat the Air fryer to 355 degrees F and grease an Air fryer basket.
2. Put the chicken breasts, mustard, paprika, Worcestershire sauce, salt, and black pepper in a food processor and pulse until minced.
3. Make 4 equal-sized patties from the mixture.

4. Place the flour in a shallow bowl and whisk the egg in a second bowl.
5. Combine dried herbs and spices in a third bowl.
6. Coat each chicken patty with flour, dip into whisked egg and then coat with breadcrumb mixture.
7. Arrange the chicken patties into the Air fryer basket in a single layer and cook for about 30 minutes, flipping once in between.
8. Place half bun in a plate, layer with lettuce leaf, patty and cheese slice.
9. Cover with bun top and dish out to serve warm.

Nutrition:

Calories: 562, Fat: 20.3g, Carbohydrates: 33g, Sugar: 3.3g, Protein: 58.7g, Sodium: 560mg

Duck Rolls

Preparation Time: 20 minutes

Cooking Time: 40 minutes

Servings: 3

Ingredients:

- 1 pound duck breast fillet, each cut into 2 pieces
- 1 small red onion, finely chopped
- 3 tablespoons fresh parsley, finely chopped
- 1 garlic clove, crushed
- 1½ teaspoons ground cumin
- 1 teaspoon ground cinnamon
- ½ teaspoon red chili powder
- 2 tablespoons olive oil
- Salt, to taste

Directions:

1. Preheat the Air fryer to 355 degrees F and grease an Air fryer basket.

2. Mix the garlic, parsley, onion, spices, and 1 tablespoon of olive oil in a bowl.
3. Make a slit in each duck piece horizontally and coat with onion mixture.
4. Roll each duck piece tightly and transfer into the Air fryer basket.
5. Cook for about 40 minutes and cut into desired size slices to serve.

Nutrition:

Calories: 239, Fats: 8.2g, Carbohydrates: 3.2g, Sugar: 0.9g, Proteins: 37.5g, Sodium: 46mg

Turkey Meatloaf

Preparation Time: 20 minutes

Cooking Time: 20 minutes

Servings: 4

Ingredients:
- 1 pound ground turkey
- 1 cup kale leaves, trimmed and finely chopped
- 1 cup onion, chopped
- ½ cup fresh breadcrumbs
- 1 cup Monterey Jack cheese, grated
- 2 garlic cloves, minced
- ¼ cup salsa verde
- 1 teaspoon red chili powder
- ½ teaspoon ground cumin
- ½ teaspoon dried oregano, crushed
- Salt and ground black pepper, as required

Directions:

1. Preheat the Air fryer to 400 degrees F and grease an Air fryer basket.
2. Mix all the ingredients in a bowl and divide the turkey mixture into 4 equal-sized portions.
3. Shape each into a mini loaf and arrange the loaves into the Air fryer basket.
4. Cook for about 20 minutes and dish out to serve warm.

Nutrition:

Calories: 435, Fat: 23.1g, Carbohydrates: 18.1g, Sugar: 3.6g, Protein: 42.2g, Sodium: 641mg

Fried Chicken Thighs

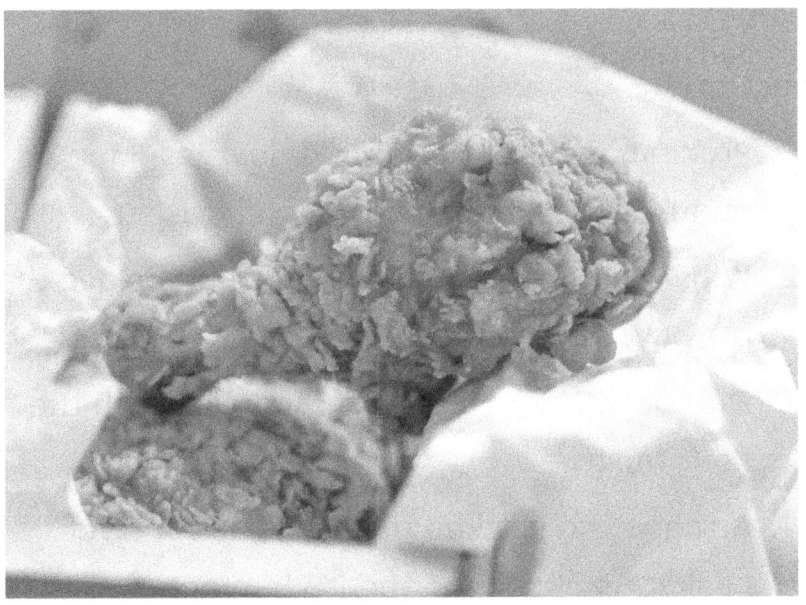

Preparation Time: 10 minutes

Cooking Time: 25 minutes

Servings: 4

Ingredients:

- ½ cup almond flour
- 1 egg beaten
- 4 small chicken thighs

- 1½ tablespoons Old Bay Cajun Seasoning
- 1 teaspoon seasoning salt

Directions:

1. Preheat the Air fryer to 400 degrees F for 3 minutes and grease an Air fryer basket.
2. Whisk the egg in a shallow bowl and place the old bay, flour and salt in another bowl.
3. Dip the chicken in the egg and coat with the flour mixture.
4. Arrange the chicken thighs in the Air fryer basket and cook for about 25 minutes.
5. Dish out in a platter and serve warm.

Nutrition:

Calories: 180, Fat: 20g, Carbohydrates: 3g, Sugar: 1.2g, Protein: 21g, Sodium: 686mg

Sesame Chicken

Preparation Time: 30 minutes

Servings: 4

Ingredients:

- 2 lbs. chicken breasts; skinless, boneless and cubed
- 1/2 cup soy sauce
- 1/2 cup honey
- 1 tbsp. olive oil
- 2 tsp. sesame oil
- 1/4 tsp. red pepper flakes
- 1/2 cup yellow onion; chopped.
- 2 garlic cloves; minced
- 1 tbsp. sesame seeds; toasted
- Salt and black pepper to taste

Directions:

1. Heat up the oil in a pan that fits your air fryer oil over medium heat.

2. Add the chicken, toss and brown for 3 minutes
3. Add the onions, garlic, salt and pepper; stir and cook for 2 minutes more.
4. Add the soy sauce, sesame oil, honey and pepper flakes; toss well
5. Place the pan in the fryer and cook at 380°F for 15 minutes
6. Top with the sesame seeds and toss. Divide between plates and serve.

Meatloaf

Preparation Time: 10 minutes

Cooking Time: 28 minutes

Serve: 8

Ingredients:

- 1 egg
- 1 tsp chili powder
- 1 tsp garlic powder

- 1 tsp garlic, minced
- 2 lbs ground turkey
- 2 oz BBQ sauce, sugar-free
- 1 tsp ground mustard
- 1 tbsp onion, minced
- 1 cup cheddar cheese, shredded
- 1 tsp salt

Directions:
1. Preheat the air fryer to 370 °F.
2. In a large bowl, combine together all ingredients then transfer into the silicon loaf pan.
3. Place loaf pan in the air fryer and cook for 25-28 minutes.
4. Serve and enjoy.

Nutrition:

Calories 301, Fat 17 g, Carbohydrates 3 g, Sugar 2.2 g, Protein 35.5 g, Cholesterol 150 mg

Chili Garlic Chicken Wings

Preparation Time: 10 minutes

Cooking Time: 35 minutes

Serve: 4

Ingredients:

- 2 lbs chicken wings
- 1/8 tsp paprika

- 1/2 cup coconut flour
- 2 tsp seasoned salt
- 1/4 tsp garlic powder
- 1/4 tsp chili powder

Directions:

1. Preheat the air fryer to 370 °F.
2. In a large bowl, add all ingredients except chicken wings and mix well.
3. Add chicken wings into the bowl coat well.
4. Spray air fryer basket with cooking spray.
5. Add chicken wings into the air fryer basket. (In batches)
6. Cook for 35-40 minutes. Shake halfway through.
7. Serve and enjoy.

Nutrition:

Calories 440, Fat 17.1 g, Carbohydrates 1 g, Sugar 0.2 g, Protein 65 g, Cholesterol 200 mg

Pesto Coated Rack of Lamb

Preparation Time: 15 minutes

Cooking Time: 15 minutes

Servings: 4

Ingredients:

- ½ bunch fresh mint
- 1: 1½-poundsrack of lamb
- 1 garlic clove

- ¼ cup extra-virgin olive oil
- ½ tablespoon honey
- Salt and black pepper, to taste

Directions:

1. Preheat the Air fryer to 200 degrees F and grease an Air fryer basket.
2. Put the mint, garlic, oil, honey, salt, and black pepper in a blender and pulse until smooth to make pesto.
3. Coat the rack of lamb with this pesto on both sides and arrange in the Air fryer basket.
4. Cook for about 15 minutes and cut the rack into individual chops to serve.

Nutrition:

Calories: 406, Fat: 27.7g, Carbohydrates: 2.9g, Sugar: 2.2g, Protein: 34.9g, Sodium: 161mg

Beef and Veggie Spring Rolls

Preparation Time: 10 minutes

Cooking Time: 14 minutes

Servings: 8

Ingredients:

- 7-ounce ground beef
- 2-ounce Asian rice noodles, soaked in warm water, drained and cut into small lengths
- 1 small onion, chopped
- 1 cup fresh mixed vegetables
- 1 packet spring roll skins
- 2 tablespoons olive oil
- Salt and black pepper, to taste

Directions:

1. Preheat the Air fryer to 350 degrees F and grease an Air fryer basket.
2. Heat olive oil in a pan and add the onion and garlic.

3. Sauté for about 5 minutes and stir in the beef.
4. Cook for about 5 minutes and add vegetables and soy sauce.
5. Cook for about 7 minutes and stir in the noodles.
6. Place the spring rolls skin onto a smooth surface and put the filling mixture diagonally in it.
7. Fold in both sides to seal properly and brush with oil.
8. Arrange the rolls in batches in the Air fryer basket and cook for about 14 minutes, tossing in between.
9. Cook for about 15 minutes, flipping once in between and dish out in a platter.

Nutrition:

Calories: 147, Fat: 5.4g, Carbohydrates: 15.9g, Sugar: 0.6g, Protein: 8.7g, Sodium: 302mg

Ham Pinwheels

Preparation Time: 15 minutes

Cooking Time: 11 minutes

Servings: 4

Ingredients:

- 1 puff pastry sheet
- 10 ham slices
- 1 cup Gruyere cheese, shredded plus more for sprinkling
- 4 teaspoons Dijon mustard

Directions:

1. Preheat the Air fryer to 375 degrees F and grease an Air fryer basket.
2. Place the puff pastry onto a smooth surface and spread evenly with the mustard.
3. Top with the ham and ¾ cup cheese and roll the puff pastry.
4. Wrap the roll in plastic wrap and freeze for about 30 minutes.

5. Remove from the freezer and slice into ½-inch rounds.
6. Arrange the pinwheels in the Air fryer basket and cook for about 8 minutes.
7. Top with remaining cheese and cook for 3 more minutes.
8. Dish out in a platter and serve warm.

Nutrition:

Calories: 294, Fat: 19.4g, Carbohydrates: 8.4g, Sugar: 0.2g, Protein: 20.8g, Sodium: 1090mg

Vegetable Cane

Preparation time: 10-20 minutes,

Cooking time: more than 60 minutes;

Serve: 4

Ingredients:
- 2 calf legs
- 4 carrots
- 4 medium potatoes
- 1 clove garlic
- 300ml Broth
- Leave to taste
- Pepper to taste

Directions:
1. Place the ears, garlic, and half of the broth in the greased basket.
2. Set the temperature to 180 ^{0}C.
3. Cook the stems for 40 minutes, turning them in the middle of cooking.

4. Add the vegetables in pieces, salt, pepper, pour the rest of the broth and cook for another 50 minutes (time may vary depending on the size of the hocks).
5. Mix the vegetables and the ears 2 to 3 times during cooking.

Nutrition:

Calories 7.9, Fat 0.49g, Carbohydrate 0.77g, Sugar 0.49g, Protein 0.08mg, Cholesterol 0mg

Basil Beef Roast

Preparation Time: 60 minutes

Servings: 6

Ingredients:

- 1½ lbs. beef roast
- 2 garlic cloves; minced
- 2 carrots; sliced
- 11 cup beef stock
- tbsp. basil; dried
- Salt and black pepper to taste

Directions:

1. In a pan that fits your air fryer, combine all ingredients well.
2. Place the pan in the fryer and cook at 390 °F for 55 minutes
3. Slice the roast, divide it and the carrots between plates and serve with cooking juices drizzled on top.

Lamb Loin Chops with Garlic

Servings: 4

Preparation Time: 10 minutes

Cooking Time: 30 minutes

Ingredients

- 3 garlic cloves, crushed
- 1 tablespoon fresh lemon juice
- 1 tablespoon Za'atar*
- 1 teaspoon olive oil
- Kosher salt and ground black pepper, as required
- 8: 3½-ouncesbone-in lamb loin chops, trimmed

Directions:

1. In a large bowl, mix together the garlic, lemon juice, oil, Za'atar, salt, and black pepper.
2. Add chops and generously coat with the mixture.
3. Set the temperature of air fryer to 400 degrees F. Grease an air fryer basket.

4. Arrange chops into the prepared air fryer basket in a single layer in 2 batches.
5. Air Fry for about 15 minutes, flipping once after 4-5 minutes per side.
6. Remove from air fryer and transfer the chops onto plates.
7. Serve hot.

Nutrition:

Calories: 433, Carbohydrate: 0.6g, Protein: 64.1g, Fat: 17.6g, Sugar: 0.2g, Sodium: 201mg

(Note: Za'atar* - Za'atar is generally made with ground dried thyme, oregano, marjoram, or some combination thereof, mixed with toasted sesame seeds, and salt, though other spices such as sumac might also be added. Some commercial varieties also include roasted flour.

Fried Pork

Preparation time: 10 – 20 minutes,

Cooking time: 15 minutes;

Serve: 4

Ingredients

- 300 g pork loin
- 2 egg yolks
- 4 tsp Worcestershire sauce:
- Taste Flour

- Gusto breadcrumbs
- Salt to taste

Directions:

1. Put the egg yolk, Worcestershire sauce and some flour (to thicken the sauce) in a bowl.
2. Cut the meat into pieces, lightly salt, and then pass it first in the sauce (previously prepared) and in breadcrumbs.
3. Grease the basket of the air fryer.
4. Preheat the air fryer for 1 minute at 200 °C.
5. Add the pork and cook for 10 minutes, turning the meat halfway through cooking.

Nutrition:

Calories 178, Fat 11.89g, Carbohydrates 0g, Sugars 0g, Protein 16.66g, Cholesterol 51mg

Roasted Veggie Bowl

Preparation Time: 25 minutes

Servings: 2

Ingredients:

- ¼ medium white onion; peeled.and sliced ¼-inch thick
- 1 cup broccoli florets
- ½ medium green bell pepper; seeded and sliced ¼-inch thick
- 1 cup quartered Brussels sprouts
- ½ cup cauliflower florets
- 1 tbsp. coconut oil
- ½ tsp. garlic powder.
- ½ tsp. cumin
- 2 tsp. chili powder

Directions:

1. Toss all ingredients together in a large bowl until vegetables are fully coated with oil and seasoning. Pour vegetables into the air fryer

basket.

2. Adjust the temperature to 360 Degrees F and set the timer for 15 minutes. Shake two or three times during cooking. Serve warm.

Nutrition:

Calories: 121; Protein: 4.3g; Fiber: 5.2g; Fat: 7.1g; Carbs: 13.1g

Wine Infused Mushrooms

Servings: 6

Preparation Time: 15 minutes

Cooking Time: 32 minutes

Ingredients

- 1 tablespoon butter
- 2 teaspoons Herbs de Provence
- 2 pounds fresh mushrooms, quartered
- ½ teaspoon garlic powder
- 2 tablespoons white vermouth*

Directions:

1. Set the temperature of air fryer to 320 degrees F.
2. In an air fryer pan, mix together the butter, Herbs de Provence, and garlic powder and air fry for about 2 minutes.
3. Stir in the mushrooms and air fry for about 25 minutes.

4. Stir in the vermouth and air fry for 5 more minutes.
5. Remove from air fryer and transfer the mushrooms onto serving plates.
6. Serve hot.

Nutrition:

Calories: 54, Carbohydrate: 5.3g, Protein: 4.8g, Fat: 2.4g, Sugar: 2.7g, Sodium: 23mg

(Note: White vermouth* - Vermouth is an aromatized, fortified white wine flavored with various botanicals and sometimes colored. The modern versions of the beverage were first produced in the mid to late 18th century in Turin, Italy.

Cheesy Spinach

Servings: 3

Preparation Time: 15 minutes

Cooking Time: 15 minutes

Ingredients

- 1: 10-ounces package frozen spinach, thawed
- ½ cup onion, chopped
- 2 teaspoons garlic, minced
- 4 ounces cream cheese, chopped
- ½ teaspoon ground nutmeg
- ¼ cup Parmesan cheese, shredded
- Salt and ground black pepper, as required

Directions:

1. In a bowl, mix well spinach, onion, garlic, cream cheese, nutmeg, salt, and black pepper.
2. Set the temperature of air fryer to 350 degrees F. Grease an air fryer pan.
3. Place spinach mixture into the prepared air fryer pan.

4. Air fry for about 10 minutes.
5. Remove from air fryer and stir the mixture well.
6. Sprinkle the spinach mixture evenly with Parmesan cheese.
7. Now, set the temperature of air fryer to 400 degrees F and air fry for 5 more minutes.
8. Remove from air fryer and transfer the spinach mixture onto serving plates.
9. Serve hot.

Nutrition:

Calories: 194, Carbohydrate: 7.3g, Protein: 8.4g, Fat: 15.5g, Sugar: 1.4g, Sodium: 351mg

Grilled Chicken with Bold Dressing

Servings: 8

Cooking Time: 40 minutes

Ingredients:

- 1 dried Mexican chili, shredded
- ½ teaspoon crushed red pepper flakes
- ¾ cup fresh cilantro
- ¼ cup chopped oregano
- 1 teaspoon lime zest
- 4 pounds chicken breasts
- Salt and pepper to taste

Directions

1. Place all ingredients in a Ziploc bag and give a good shake.
2. Allow to marinate in the fridge for at least 2 hours.
3. Preheat the air fryer at 375 degrees F.

4. Place the grill pan accessory in the air fryer.
5. Grill for at least 40 minutes making sure to flip the chicken every 10 minutes for even grilling.

Nutrition

522. Calories: 394; Carbs:0.9 g; Protein: 47.4g; Fat: 21g

Indian Spiced Chicken, Eggplant, and Tomato Skewers

Servings: 4

Cooking Time: 25 minutes

Ingredients:
- 4 cloves of garlic, minced
- 1-inch ginger, grated
- 1 can coconut milk
- 3 teaspoons lime zest
- 2 tablespoons fresh lime juice
- 2 tablespoons tomato paste
- 1 ½ teaspoon ground turmeric
- ¼ teaspoon cayenne pepper
- ¼ teaspoon ground cardamom
- 2 pounds boneless chicken breasts, cut into cubes
- 1 medium eggplant, cut into cubes
- 1 onion, cut into wedges
- 1 cup cherry tomatoes

- Salt and pepper to taste

Directions

1. In a bowl, place the garlic, ginger, coconut milk, lime zest, lime juice, tomato paste, salt, pepper, turmeric, cayenne pepper, cardamom, and chicken breasts. Allow to marinate in the fridge for at least for 2 hours.
2. Preheat the air fryer at 375 degree F.
3. Place the grill pan accessory in the air fryer.
4. Skewer the chicken cubes with eggplant, onion, and cherry tomatoes on bamboo skewers.
5. Place on the grill pan and cook for 25 minutes making sure to flip the skewers every 5 minutes for even cooking.

Nutrition

Calories: 479; Carbs:19.7 g; Protein: 55.2g; Fat: 20.6g

Grilled Chicken with Shishito Peppers

Servings: 6

Cooking Time: 30 minutes

Ingredients:

- 3 pounds chicken wings
- 2 tablespoons sesame oil
- 1 ½ cups shishito peppers, pureed
- Salt and pepper to taste

Directions

1. Place all ingredients in a Ziploc bag and allow to marinate for at least 2 hours in the fridge.
2. Preheat the air fryer at 375 degrees F.
3. Place the grill pan accessory in the air fryer.
4. Grill for at least 30 minutes flipping the chicken every 5 minutes and basting with the remaining sauce.

Nutrition

Calories: 333; Carbs: 1.7g; Protein: 50.2g; Fat: 12.6g

Stuffed Mushrooms with Sour Cream

Preparation Time: 15 minutes

Cooking Time: 8 minutes

Servings: 12

Ingredients:

- ¼ orange bell pepper, diced
- ¾ cup Cheddar cheese, shredded
- 12 mushrooms caps, stems diced

- ½ onion, diced
- ½ small carrot, diced
- ¼ cup sour cream

Directions:

1. Preheat the Air fryer to 350 degrees F and grease a baking tray.
2. Place mushroom stems, onion, orange bell pepper and carrot over medium heat in a skillet.
3. Cook for about 5 minutes until softened and stir in ½ cup Cheddar cheese and sour cream.
4. Stuff this mixture in the mushroom caps and arrange them on the baking tray.
5. Top with rest of the cheese and place the baking tray in the Air fryer basket.
6. Cook for about 8 minutes until cheese is melted and serve warm.

Nutrition:

Calories: 43, Fat: 3.1g, Carbohydrates: 1.7g, Sugar: 1g, Protein: 2.4g, Sodium: 55mg

Air Fried Chicken Tenders

Preparation Time: 15 minutes

Cooking Time: 10 minutes

Servings: 4

Ingredients:

- 12 oz chicken breasts, cut into tenders
- 1 egg white
- 1/8 cup flour
- ½ cup panko bread crumbs

- Salt and black pepper, to taste

Directions:

1. Preheat the Air fryer to 350 degrees F and grease an Air fryer basket.
2. Season the chicken tenders with salt and black pepper.
3. Coat the chicken tenders with flour, then dip in egg whites and then dredge in the panko bread crumbs.
4. Arrange in the Air fryer basket and cook for about 10 minutes.
5. Dish out in a platter and serve warm.

Nutrition:

Calories: 220, Fat: 17.1g, Carbohydrates: 6g, Sugar: 3.5g, Protein: 12.8g, Sodium: 332mg

French Toast Bites

Preparation Time: 5 minutes

Cooking Time: 15 minutes

Servings: 8

Ingredients:

- 3 eggs
- Almond milk

- Cinnamon
- Sweetener
- 4 pieces wheat bread

Directions:

1. Preheat the air fryer oven to 360 degrees.
2. Whisk eggs and thin out with almond milk.
3. Mix 1/3 cup of sweetener with lots of cinnamon.
4. Tear bread in half, ball up pieces and press together to form a ball.
5. Soak bread balls in egg and then roll into cinnamon sugar, making sure to thoroughly coat.
6. Place coated bread balls into the air fryer oven and bake 15 minutes.

Nutrition:

Calories – 289, Protein – 0 g., Fat – 11 g., Carbs – 17 g.

Currant Cream

Preparation Time: 35 minutes

Servings: 4

Ingredients:

- 7 cups red currants
- 6 sage leaves
- 1 cup water
- 1 cup swerve

Directions:

1. In a pan that fits your air fryer, mix all the ingredients, toss, put the pan in the fryer and cook at 330 °F for 30 minutes
2. Discard sage leaves, divide into cups and serve cold.

Nutrition:

Calories: 171; Fat: 4g; Fiber: 2g; Carbs: 3g; Protein: 6g

Marshmallow Pastries

Preparation Time: 20 minutes

Cooking Time: 5 minutes

Servings: 8

Ingredients:

- 4-ounce butter, melted
- ½ cup chunky peanut butter
- 8 phyllo pastry sheets, thawed
- 8 teaspoons marshmallow fluff
- Pinch of salt

Directions:

1. Preheat the Air fryer to 360 degree F and grease an Air fryer basket.
2. Brush butter over 1 filo pastry sheet and top with a second filo sheet.
3. Brush butter over second filo pastry sheet and repeat with all the remaining sheets.

4. Cut the phyllo layers in 8 strips and put 1 tablespoon of peanut butter and 1 teaspoon of marshmallow fluff on the underside of a filo strip.
5. Fold the tip of the sheet over the filling to form a triangle and fold repeatedly in a zigzag manner.
6. Arrange the pastries into the Air fryer basket and cook for about 5 minutes.
7. Season with a pinch of salt and serve warm.

Nutrition:

Calories: 283, Fat: 20.6g, Carbohydrates: 20.2g, Sugar: 3.4g, Protein: 6g, Sodium: 320mg

Double Layer Lemon Bars

Preparation Time: 10 minutes

Cooking Time: 25 minutes

Servings: 6

Ingredients:

For the crust:

- 1 cup coconut flour, sifted
- 1 tablespoon butter, melted

For the lemon topping:

- 3 eggs
- 2 teaspoons coconut flour, sifted

For the crust:

- ½ cup coconut oil, melted
- Swerve, to taste
- A pinch of salt

For the lemon topping:

- Swerve, to taste
- ½ cup fresh lemon juice
- 2 teaspoons lemon zest

Directions:

1. Preheat the Air fryer to 350 degrees F and grease a 6-inch baking pan lightly.
2. Mix butter, swerve, salt, and oil in a bowl until foamy.
3. Stir in the coconut flour and mix until a smooth dough is formed.
4. Place the dough into the baking pan and press it thoroughly.
5. Transfer into the Air fryer and cook for about 8 minutes.
6. Meanwhile, whisk eggs with swerve, lemon zest, coconut flour and lemon juice in a bowl and mix well until smooth.
7. Pour this filling into the air fried crust and place into the Air fryer.
8. Set the Air fryer to 370 degrees F and cook for about 23 minutes.
9. Cut into slices and serve.

Nutrition:

Calories: 301, Fat: 12.2g, Carbohydrates: 2.5g, Sugar: 1.4g, Protein: 8.8g, Sodium: 276mg

Chocolate Mug Cake

Preparation Time: 15 minutes

Cooking Time: 13 minutes

Servings: 1

Ingredients:

- ¼ cup self-rising flour
- 5 tablespoons caster sugar
- 3 tablespoons coconut oil
- 1 tablespoon cocoa powder

- 3 tablespoons whole milk

Directions:

1. In a shallow mug, add all the ingredients and mix until well combined.
2. Press "Power Button" of Air Fry Oven and turn the dial to select the "Air Fry" mode.
3. Press the Time button and again turn the dial to set the cooking time to 13 minutes.
4. Now push the Temp button and rotate the dial to set the temperature at 392 degrees F.
5. Press "Start/Pause" button to start.
6. When the unit beeps to show that it is preheated, open the lid.
7. Arrange the mug in "Air Fry Basket" and insert in the oven.
8. Place the mug onto a wire rack to cool slightly before serving.

Nutrition:

Calories – 729 Protein – 5.7 g.Fat – 43.3 g.Carbs – 88.8 g.

Blueberry Cake

Preparation Time: 10 minutes

Cooking Time: 25 minutes

Servings: 6

Ingredients:

- 3 eggs
- 1 cup almond flour
- 1 stick butter, room temperature

- 1/3 cup blueberries
- 1½ teaspoons baking powder
- ½ cup sour cream
- 2/3 cup swerve
- 2 teaspoons vanilla

Directions:

1. Preheat the Air fryer to 370 degrees F and grease a baking pan lightly.
2. Mix all the ingredients in a bowl except blueberries.
3. Pour the batter in the baking pan and fold in the blueberries.
4. Mix well and transfer the pan in the Air fryer basket.
5. Cook for about 25 minutes and cut into slices to serve.

Nutrition:

Calories: 323, Fat: 14g, Carbohydrates: 5.3g, Sugar: 1.4g, Protein: 4.6g, Sodium: 92mg

Cinnamon Rolls

Preparation Time: 12 minutes

Servings: 8

Ingredients:
- 1 lb. bread dough
- 3/4 cup brown sugar
- 1/4 cup butter; melted
- 1½ tbsp. cinnamon; ground

Directions:
1. Roll the dough on a floured working surface, shape a rectangle and brush with the butter.
2. In a bowl, combine the cinnamon and sugar and then sprinkle this over the dough
3. Roll the dough into a log, seal, cut into 8 pieces and leave the rolls to rise for 2 hours
4. Place the rolls in your air fryer's basket and cook at 350 °F for 5 minutes on each side. Serve warm and enjoy!

Raspberry-Coconut Cupcake

Servings: 6

Cooking Time: 30 minutes

Ingredients

- ½ cup butter
- ½ teaspoon salt
- ¾ cup erythritol
- 1 cup almond milk, unsweetened

- 1 cup coconut flour
- 1 tablespoon baking powder
- 3 teaspoons vanilla extract
- 7 large eggs, beaten

Directions:

1. Preheat the air fryer for 5 minutes.
2. Mix all ingredients using a hand mixer.
3. Pour into hard cupcake molds.
4. Place in the air fryer basket.
5. Bake for 30 minutes at 350 degrees F or until a toothpick inserted in the middle comes out clean.
6. Bake by batches if possible.
7. Allow to chill before serving.

Nutrition:

Calories: 235; Carbohydrates: 7.4g; Protein: 3.8g; Fat: 21.1g

Apple-Toffee Upside-Down Cake

Servings: 9

Cooking Time: 30 minutes

Ingredients

- ¼ cup almond butter
- ¼ cup sunflower oil
- ¾ cup + 3 tablespoon coconut sugar
- ½ cup walnuts, chopped
- ¾ cup water
- 1 ½ teaspoon mixed spice
- 1 lemon, zest
- 1 cup plain flour
- 1 teaspoon baking soda
- 1 teaspoon vinegar
- 3 baking apples, cored and sliced

Directions:

1. Preheat the air fryer to 390 degrees F.
2. In a skillet, melt the almond butter and 3 tablespoons sugar. Pour the mixture over a

baking dish that will fit in the air fryer. Arrange the slices of apples on top. Set aside.

3. In a mixing bowl, combine flour, ¾ cup sugar, and baking soda. Add the mixed spice.
4. In another bowl, mix the oil, water, vinegar, and lemon zest. Stir in the chopped walnuts.
5. Combine the wet ingredients to the dry ingredients until well combined.
6. Pour over the tin with apple slices.
7. Bake for 30 minutes or until a toothpick inserted comes out clean.

Nutrition:

Calories: 335; Carbohydrates: 39.6g; Protein: 3.8g; Fat: 17.9g

Strawberry Pop Tarts

Servings: 6

Cooking Time: 25 minutes

Ingredients

- 1 oz reduced-fat Philadelphia cream cheese
- 1 tsp cornstarch
- 1 tsp stevia

- 1 tsp sugar sprinkles
- 1/2 cup plain, non-fat vanilla Greek yogurt
- 1/3 cup low-sugar strawberry preserves
- 2 refrigerated pie crusts
- olive oil or coconut oil spray

Directions:

1. Cut pie crusts into 6 equal rectangles.
2. In a bowl, mix cornstarch and preserves. Add preserves in middle of crust. Fold over crust. Crimp edges with fork to seal. Repeat process for remaining crusts.
3. Lightly grease baking pan of air fryer with cooking spray. Add pop tarts in single layer. Cook in batches for 8 minutes at 370 °F.
4. Meanwhile, make the frosting by mixing stevia, cream cheese, and yogurt in a bowl. Spread on top of cooked pop tart and add sugar sprinkles.
5. Serve and enjoy.

Nutrition:

Calories: 317; Carbs: 34.8g; Protein: 4.7g; Fat: 17.6g

Gluten Free Chocó Lava Cake

Preparation Time: 15 minutes

Servings: 2

Ingredients:

- 1 egg
- 1/2 tsp baking powder
- 1 tbsp coconut oil, melted
- 1 tbsp flax meal
- 1/8 tsp stevia
- 2 tbsp erythritol
- 2 tbsp cocoa powder
- 2 tbsp water
- 1/8 tsp vanilla
- Pinch of salt

Directions:

1. Spray two ramekins with cooking spray and set aside.
2. Add all ingredients to the bowl and whisk well.

3. Preheat the air fryer to 176 C/ 350 F for a minute.
4. Pour batter into the prepared ramekins. Place ramekins into the air fryer basket and cook for 8-9 minutes.
5. Serve warm and enjoy.

Nutrition Values:

Calories 122 Fat 11 g Carbohydrates 17 g Sugar 0.3 g Protein 4.5 g Cholesterol 82 mg

Cinnamon Mug Cake

Servings: 1

Preparation Time: 5 minutes

Cooking Time: 10 minutes

Ingredients

- 1/4 tsp vanilla extract
- 1 scoop vanilla protein powder
- 1/4 cup almond milk, unsweetened

- 1/2 tsp cinnamon
- 1 tsp granulated sweetener
- 1 tbsp almond flour
- 1/2 tsp baking powder

Directions

1. Add protein powder, sweetener, cinnamon, almond flour, and baking powder into the heat-safe mug and mix well.
2. Add vanilla extract and almond milk and stir well. If the batter is crumbly add more milk until formed thick batter.
3. Place mug in air fryer and cook at 200 C/ 392 F for 10 minutes
4. Serve and enjoy.

Nutrition Values:

Net Carbs: 6.3g; Calories: 180; Total Fat: 6.3g; Saturated Fat: 1.3g

Protein: 23.9g; Carbs: 8.2g

Raspberry Bites

Preparation Time: 37 minutes

Servings: 10

Ingredients:

- 1 large egg.
- 2 oz. full-fat cream cheese; softened.
- 1 cup blanched finely ground almond flour.
- 3 tbsp. granular Swerve.
- 1 tsp. baking powder.
- 10 tsp. sugar-free raspberry preserves.

Directions:

1. Mix all ingredients except preserves in a large bowl until a wet dough forms.
2. Place the bowl in the freezer for 20 minutes until dough is cool and able to roll into a ball.
3. Roll dough into ten balls and press gently in the center of each ball. Place 1 tsp. preserves in the center of each ball.

4. Cut a piece of parchment to fit your air fryer basket. Place each Danish bite on the parchment, pressing down gently to flatten the bottom.
5. Adjust the temperature to 400 Degrees F and set the timer for 7 minutes. Allow to cool completely before moving, or they will crumble.

Nutrition:

Calories: 96; Protein: 3.4g; Fiber: 1.3g; Fat: 7.7g; Carbs: 9.8g

Notes

www.ingramcontent.com/pod-product-compliance
Lightning Source LLC
Chambersburg PA
CBHW070934080526
44589CB00013B/1515